UML for the Agile Enterprise

Accelerating Software Development Through Flexible Processes and Adaptive Planning

Everett Miles

Contents

1 Introduction to Agile and UML

Agile methodologies prioritize iterative development, collaboration, and responsiveness to change. This contrasts sharply with traditional waterfall methods, where each phase must be completed before moving on. The emphasis in Agile is on delivering working software frequently, gathering feedback, and adapting to new information throughout the project lifecycle. This iterative approach allows for greater flexibility and minimizes the risk of significant deviations from the client's requirements. Consequently, projects are more likely to succeed and meet the evolving needs of stakeholders. This makes the rapid response to changing circumstances and market conditions crucial for project success, especially in a dynamic business environment.

UML, or Unified Modeling Language, is a standard visual language for specifying, visualizing, constructing, and documenting the artifacts of software systems. It's a powerful tool for understanding and communicating complex system designs. Using standardized notations ensures that everyone involved in the project – developers, designers, testers, and clients – shares a common understanding. This shared understanding is critical for minimizing miscommunications and improving overall project efficiency, leading to more consistent and successful outcomes. Furthermore, the use of visual models enhances clarity and provides a concrete representation of the system's architecture and behavior, making it easier to identify potential issues early in the development process. The combination of Agile and UML offers a powerful approach to software development. Agile's iterative nature complements UML's ability to create clear and concise models. For instance, in an Agile sprint, you might use UML diagrams to design a specific feature. This allows the team to visualize the functionality and its interaction with other parts of the system before writing any code. This approach fosters clear communication and collaboration, critical elements of successful Agile projects. The early detection of potential design flaws reduces development time and effort, ultimately leading to higher-quality products delivered faster. Consider a typical scenario. Your team is developing a mobile banking application. Using Agile, you'll break down the development into short iterations or sprints. Before starting each sprint, you could use UML use case diagrams to model the user interactions (e.g., logging in, transferring funds, checking balances). This provides a shared vision for the functionality within a sprint. Simultaneously, you might use class diagrams to model the underlying data structures and relationships between different components of the application (e.g., account, transaction, user). This visual representation aids in organizing the code and simplifies understanding the system's architecture. The visual representation is fundamental for better collaboration and communication in Agile environments.

Sequence diagrams become especially useful during the implementation phase. They illustrate the interactions between objects within a specific use case. For instance, a sequence diagram can visually depict how a user's request to transfer money flows through the system, showing the interaction between the user interface, the banking system's database, and any security protocols. These diagrams can identify potential bottlenecks or issues early on, before they become major problems in the later stages of development, facilitating faster problem resolution. The combination of the visual representation and iterative development leads to efficient problem-solving, optimizing project timeline and cost.

Agile modeling encourages continuous feedback and adaptation. After each sprint, the team reviews the implemented features and refines the UML models based on any issues encountered or new requirements identified. This iterative process ensures that the models are kept up-to-date and reflect the system's actual state, offering a continuous feedback loop for optimizing the development process. The continuous review improves the product's quality and adaptability. The combination of this process with the benefits of UML provides a continuous improvement process. This iterative feedback loop is crucial for adaptability and responsiveness to change, both hallmarks of successful Agile projects.

In short, integrating UML into an Agile workflow isn't just about creating diagrams. It's about leveraging the power of visual communication to enhance collaboration, improve understanding, reduce risks, and ultimately, deliver higher-quality software more efficiently. Using UML diagrams to communicate and validate the design facilitates a more productive and collaborative environment. This leads to smoother workflows, quicker problem-solving, and a more efficient process overall. Employing this collaborative approach not only creates a better product but also fosters a more effective and satisfied team.

1.1 Agile Principles

Embrace change. This isn't just a suggestion; it's the cornerstone of agile methodologies. Rigid plans crumble under the weight of evolving requirements and unforeseen challenges. Agile embraces the inevitable changes, allowing for adjustments throughout the development lifecycle. This adaptability leads to a more resilient and responsive software development process, better aligned with the ever-shifting demands of the market.

Individuals and interactions over processes and tools. Technology plays a role, of course, but it's the people who bring the software to life. Focus on effective communication, collaboration, and fostering a positive team environment. Encourage open dialogue, mutual respect, and a shared understanding of the project goals. Remember, the most advanced tools are useless without skilled and motivated people to wield them.

Working software over comprehensive documentation. While documentation is crucial, it shouldn't overshadow the primary goal: delivering functional software. Prioritize the creation of a working product that meets core requirements, even if it means a less detailed initial design. Iterative development allows for refinements as the project progresses, ensuring the final product aligns with user expectations and business needs. This approach emphasizes tangible results over endless theoretical discussions.

Customer collaboration over contract negotiation. Agile is about building a partnership with the customer, not just fulfilling a contract. Regular feedback loops, close collaboration, and responsive adjustments to evolving needs ensure the software meets its target audience's actual requirements. This proactive approach minimizes disagreements and ensures the final product satisfies the client's expectations. Strong communication is crucial for success.

Responding to change over following a plan. Change is inevitable. Rigid adherence to pre-defined plans often leads to frustration and delays. Agile methodologies encourage adaptability. Regularly re-evaluate the project's direction based on new information and feedback, adjusting the plan as necessary. This flexibility allows teams to pivot efficiently and create software that meets current needs and remains competitive in a dynamic environment. Prioritizing this responsiveness ensures the product's viability.

These principles, seemingly simple, form the bedrock of a truly agile approach to software development using UML. They represent a shift from traditional, rigid methodologies toward a more adaptable and collaborative process. The practical implementation of these principles, combined with the power of UML's visual modeling tools, enables teams to create higher-quality software more efficiently, and effectively respond to changes. They foster innovation and team spirit in the process of software design.

Remember, the Agile Manifesto isn't a rigid set of rules, but rather a guiding philosophy. It's a framework for approaching software development in a way that is responsive, flexible, and ultimately more successful in the long run. Understanding these five core values is paramount for any team looking to effectively utilize the UML tools and methodologies. Their successful application lies in thoughtful application and continuous adaptation.

Effective use of UML diagrams aids in achieving these principles. For instance, use case modeling helps ensure the software aligns with customer needs, facilitating customer collaboration. Iteration planning through UML models supports responding to change, while class diagrams allow for efficient design and maintainability. This integrated approach creates a synergistic effect, amplifying the benefits of both Agile and UML. The proper use of UML tools improves clarity, reduces risks and speeds up the development process.

Agile and UML together represent a powerful combination. UML provides the structure and visualization, allowing for efficient communication and collaboration, thereby supporting the Agile principles of customer collaboration and responding to change. By leveraging the strengths of both methodologies, development teams can optimize the entire software development life cycle. Effective modeling helps to decrease time to market and increases the quality of the software delivered. The success of implementing these principles depends on the team's commitment and willingness to adapt. It's an iterative process, requiring continuous learning and improvement. Embrace experimentation, embrace failure as a learning opportunity, and remember that Agile is a journey, not a destination. Success requires consistent effort, open communication, and a team spirit driven by a shared objective. Focus on making this agile approach a vital and integral part of your development process. The process requires patience and consistency, but the rewards are significant.

1.2 UML Overview

UML, or the Unified Modeling Language, isn't just a collection of diagrams; it's a powerful visual language that streamlines communication and accelerates software development, particularly within an Agile environment. Think of it as a shared vocabulary, allowing developers, designers, and stakeholders to speak the same visual language, fostering better collaboration and minimizing misunderstandings. This shared understanding dramatically reduces ambiguity, leading to more efficient development cycles and fewer costly revisions later in the process. It facilitates a common understanding of the system's structure and behavior, which is crucial for the iterative nature of Agile development.

Understanding UML's core diagrams is paramount. The most frequently used are class diagrams, which illustrate the system's static structure, showcasing classes, their attributes, and relationships. Imagine a blueprint of your software, defining the objects and how they interact. This detailed picture isn't just for developers; it's for anyone needing a clear view of the system's architecture. Use case diagrams provide a functional perspective, illustrating how users interact with the system, focusing on what the system does rather than how it does it. This is crucial for ensuring you build the right software. Sequence diagrams then delve into the dynamic behavior, mapping out interactions between objects over time, offering a chronological view of the system in action. Finally, state machine diagrams model the behavior of individual objects based on their states and transitions, essential for handling complex object interactions and responses.

Successfully utilizing UML within an Agile workflow necessitates a shift in mindset. It's not about creating perfect, exhaustive models upfront; instead, it's about iterative model refinement. Start with simple, high-level models, focusing on core functionalities. Then, as you progress through sprints, gradually elaborate those models, adding detail as required. This approach aligns perfectly with Agile's iterative nature, allowing for flexibility and adaptation to evolving requirements. Remember, your UML models should serve the Agile process, not hinder it. Overly complex diagrams can become counterproductive.

Practical application is key. Begin by identifying the core functionalities of your system. Translate these functionalities into use cases, ensuring clear definitions of actors and system interactions. These use cases will inform your class diagrams, guiding the design of your classes and their relationships. Use sequence diagrams to model complex interactions between objects within those classes, identifying potential bottlenecks or ambiguities in the design. State machine diagrams are particularly helpful when dealing with objects exhibiting varied states or behaviors. This iterative process—from identifying functionalities to designing classes and modeling interactions—ensures a cohesive and well-structured system design.

Effective Agile UML modeling is also about communication. Regularly review your models with the team, soliciting feedback and ensuring everyone is on the same page. Consider using collaborative modeling tools that allow for real-time updates and contributions. The value of UML isn't solely in the diagrams themselves, but in the discussions and shared understanding they foster among team members. These discussions can uncover potential problems early on, prevent misunderstandings, and ensure everyone is working toward the same goals. Don't consider UML as a standalone activity, but rather as an integral part of the Agile development process. It's a tool for collaboration and clarity, not an additional bureaucratic burden.

Finally, remember that UML is a tool; its effectiveness depends on how you use it. Don't be afraid to experiment and adapt your modeling approach based on your specific project requirements. Focus on creating clear, concise diagrams that effectively communicate the necessary information to your team and stakeholders. And, importantly, keep your models focused on what is essential, avoid excessive details, and continuously refine them throughout the development lifecycle. Agile principles and UML are synergistic; they complement each other, creating a powerful combination for developing successful software. The key is to use UML strategically, focusing on its value in facilitating clear communication, efficient collaboration, and the successful delivery of your project.

2 Use Case Modeling

Use Case Modeling is crucial for capturing the functional requirements of a system. It's all about understanding what the system does from the user's perspective, not how it does it. This perspective is vital, ensuring we build software that truly meets user needs and expectations. Ignoring this step often leads to costly rework later in the development cycle. A well-defined set of use cases acts as a contract between the development team and stakeholders, offering clarity on expectations and reducing misunderstandings.

Identifying actors and their interactions with the system is the first step. Actors are anything that interacts with the system, be it a user, another system, a database, or even a timer. Consider each actor's role and how they might interact with the system. A simple online banking system, for instance, might have actors such as a customer, a bank teller, and a payment gateway. Each actor would have different use cases. Think carefully about all potential interactions; even seemingly minor actions can be significant. Thorough analysis now saves significant time and effort down the line.

Use case diagrams provide a visual representation of these interactions. These diagrams are high-level overviews, showing the actors and the use cases they perform. They don't get bogged down in implementation details; instead, they focus on the 'what' rather than the 'how'. A well-constructed diagram provides an intuitive overview for both technical and non-technical stakeholders, making it a great communication tool. Simple shapes and clear connections make them easy to understand and modify. They facilitate discussion and collaboration, helping to uncover gaps and ambiguities early on. Consider using standardized notation to ensure everyone interprets the diagram correctly.

Use case descriptions delve deeper into each use case. This goes beyond the simple diagrammatic representation, detailing the flow of events for each use case. It includes pre-conditions, post-conditions, normal flows, and alternative flows. Pre-conditions are the states that must exist before the use case begins. Post-conditions are the states that will exist after the use case completes. Normal flow describes the expected sequence of events. Alternative flows detail exceptional circumstances or user choices. This detailed breakdown ensures no aspect of functionality is overlooked, contributing to a more comprehensive understanding. Detailed documentation minimizes misunderstanding and allows developers to create efficient and robust solutions.

Consider the 'withdraw cash' use case in our online banking system. The pre-condition might be that the customer is logged in. The post-condition could be that the customer's account balance is updated, and a transaction record is created. The normal flow might involve selecting the withdrawal option, specifying the amount, entering the PIN, and receiving the cash. An alternative flow could be what happens if the customer enters the wrong PIN three times. Use clear, unambiguous language in your descriptions; aim for precision.

Remember to keep the use cases concise and focused. Avoid overly complex scenarios that would overwhelm the readers. Prioritize clarity; the aim is for easy understanding. Overly complex descriptions make the model difficult to use, reducing its effectiveness. Use case descriptions should be easily understandable by both developers and stakeholders and shouldn't require specialized technical knowledge. This approach ensures everyone involved in the project understands its requirements, promoting clear communication across the team.

Using use case modeling effectively can significantly improve the quality and efficiency of software development. By thoroughly defining actors and use cases, you establish a strong foundation for the entire development process, reducing the risk of costly errors and rework down the line. The visual representation offered by use case diagrams enhances communication and collaboration among stakeholders, ensuring that everyone is on the same page regarding the system's functionality. The detailed descriptions of use cases provide a comprehensive guide for developers, ensuring that no aspect of the functionality is overlooked. In short, investing time in robust use case modeling is an investment in a smoother and more successful software development process.

2.1 Identifying Actors and Use Cases

Identifying actors within a system is crucial for effective use case modeling. These actors represent anyone or anything that interacts with the system, be it a human user, another software system, a hardware device, or even a timer. Think about who or what initiates actions within your application; these are your primary actors. Remember, accurately identifying actors lays the groundwork for a comprehensive understanding of system functionality. This initial step prevents misunderstandings and ensures the system addresses the real-world needs it's intended to serve. The clarity this provides significantly improves the entire development process, ultimately leading to a more user-friendly and efficient final product.

Defining use cases, on the other hand, involves specifying the individual functions the system performs. Each use case describes a specific interaction between an actor and the system, resulting in a tangible outcome. For instance, a banking application might have use cases such as "withdraw cash," "deposit funds," and "transfer money." Each use case represents a distinct user goal and should be clearly described with a unique identifier and a concise summary. This detailed description will later enable you to design the system effectively and efficiently, minimizing any ambiguity that may arise later in development. The detailed specification of use cases is essential for a successful outcome.

Consider a simple e-commerce system. Here, actors might include the customer, the administrator, and a payment gateway. The customer actor interacts with the system to browse products, add items to a cart, and make a purchase. The administrator manages products, inventory, and user accounts. The payment gateway processes transactions. These actors perform distinct actions within the system and their interactions drive its functionality. Carefully identifying these actors early in the process helps create a well-structured model, ultimately leading to the creation of a system that accurately reflects user requirements. Thorough planning ensures a superior final product.

Use cases for this e-commerce system might include "Browse Products," "Add to Cart," "Checkout," "Manage Inventory," and "Process Payment." Each use case encapsulates a specific interaction, enabling a granular analysis of system requirements. Clearly defined use cases, like these, act as building blocks for the system design, providing detailed information about the functions and interactions needed. This detailed approach provides a robust foundation for the development process. Furthermore, a precise definition aids in understanding the scope of work, and in the development of a system that meets expectations from the outset.

Effective use case modeling, through a careful identification of actors and use cases, ensures that the system development remains focused and efficiently addresses its intended goals. The entire process is significantly streamlined and is more likely to result in a system which accurately reflects the user's needs. It fosters clear communication among developers and stakeholders, ensuring everyone is on the same page about the system's intended functionality. This clear understanding of requirements translates into efficient code development and a better overall user experience. A well-defined model allows for changes and iterations throughout the development lifecycle, enhancing adaptability in the agile environment. The result is a more flexible and maintainable system, well equipped for future adaptation and enhancement.

The key to successful use case modeling lies in collaboration. Involving users and stakeholders throughout the process allows for the early identification and resolution of ambiguities. This collaborative approach ensures the resulting system directly addresses the needs of those who will ultimately be using it. This iterative process, typical of Agile methodologies, ensures that the model evolves along with the project's understanding of the requirements. It encourages constant feedback, resulting in a product closely aligned with its end purpose, leading to increased user satisfaction. This collaborative environment ensures efficiency and allows for a superior product.

2.2 Use Case Diagrams

Use case diagrams offer a powerful way to visually represent the interactions between users (or actors) and a system. They're essential for capturing functional requirements, ensuring that your software meets the needs of its intended audience. Think of them as a blueprint for how your software will be used, not how it's built. This focus on functionality helps to keep the design focused on user needs and avoid getting bogged down in technical details too early in the development process. They're incredibly useful for communication, especially with clients who may not have a technical background. A well-drawn diagram can bridge the gap between technical specifications and the user experience.

Creating a use case diagram starts with identifying the actors. These are the entities that interact with the system—people, other systems, or even external devices. For example, in an online banking system, the actors might include a customer, a bank teller, and an external payment processor. Each actor will have specific interactions with the system, which will be represented by use cases. Clearly defining these actors is crucial to understanding the scope of your software. Overlooking an actor can lead to significant design flaws later.

Next, you need to pinpoint the use cases, which represent the specific functions or tasks the system performs. Each use case should describe a complete interaction from the user's perspective. A use case for our online banking system might be "transfer funds," "pay bills," or "check account balance." These are self-contained actions that users undertake within the system. It is important to be detailed when defining these, striving for clarity and avoiding ambiguity. A poorly defined use case can lead to misunderstandings and ultimately, a poorly built system. Don't rush this process.

The diagrams themselves use simple notation: actors are usually represented by stick figures, while use cases are represented by ovals. Lines connect the actors to the use cases they participate in. This visual representation allows stakeholders to quickly grasp the overall functionality of the system without getting lost in complex technical details. Simplicity is key here, and a cluttered diagram is counterproductive. Keep it clean and easy to understand. A well-structured diagram will speak volumes.

Remember that use case diagrams are not just for the technical team. They are a crucial communication tool for collaborating with stakeholders, clients, and other non-technical team members. By providing a clear, visual representation of how the system will be used, you can ensure everyone is on the same page. Early feedback from these stakeholders can prevent costly redesigns down the line. This inclusive approach is a significant advantage of UML for agile development, allowing for adaptability and reducing the likelihood of building features no one needs or will use.

While use case diagrams focus on the 'what' of the system, they lay the foundation for subsequent modeling activities. For instance, they inform the design of class diagrams, which detail the system's internal structure and objects. Similarly, sequence diagrams, which illustrate the flow of interactions, can be derived from the use cases. It's a stepping stone towards more complex UML diagrams, all connected by a focus on the system's functional requirements. This methodical progression is crucial for effective agile development. It's about building a stable architecture, one step at a time.

Finally, remember that creating a use case diagram is an iterative process. As you refine your understanding of the system's requirements, the diagram will evolve. This reflects the inherent flexibility of agile methodologies. You will likely make changes as you get feedback and as your understanding of the project improves. Don't be afraid to revise and update your diagram as the project progresses. It's a living document, adapting to the changing requirements of the development cycle. Consider it a dynamic tool, always reflecting the current state of understanding. The iterative nature of its development parallels the iterative nature of agile development. Embrace this adaptability.

2.3 Use Case Descriptions

A well-written use case description is crucial for effective communication within your Agile team and with stakeholders. It's more than just a list of steps; it's a detailed narrative that clearly outlines the interaction between an actor and the system. Imagine it as a mini-story, focused on a single function of your software. Consider all aspects: from the user's initial action to the system's response and the resulting state. This ensures everyone understands the intended functionality. This prevents misunderstandings, saving time and resources down the line.

Think of the actor, the user or external system interacting with your software. Clearly define who they are and what their goals are within the specific use case. Are they a customer placing an order, an administrator managing user accounts, or a payment gateway processing a transaction? Describing the actor's role and motivation brings the use case to life and makes it relatable for everyone. Avoid vague descriptions. Be specific.

The goal is to articulate the user's purpose clearly. What problem are they trying to solve by using this particular function of your application? Why are they interacting with the system in this way? Understanding the user's intent shapes the design of the use case and ensures that the functionality fulfills its purpose. A defined goal will also help you establish the boundaries of your use case, so it doesn't try to do too much at once.

The preconditions define the state of the system before the use case begins. What must be true or already exist for this use case to even start? For instance, a user must be logged in to place an order; a valid product must be selected; a payment method must be chosen. Defining these beforehand ensures the use case starts from a known and valid state, preventing errors and unexpected behavior. It streamlines the process, making it straightforward and efficient.

The postconditions describe the state of the system after the use case has completed successfully. What changes have occurred? Has an order been placed and confirmed? Has a new user account been created? Have payment details been processed? Clearly outlining these postconditions guarantees the system functions as intended and that the use case achieved its goal. This helps to verify successful completion, which is key for testing.

Now, consider the main success scenario. This outlines the ideal path the user follows to achieve their goal. This is the "happy path" — the most straightforward, successful completion of the use case. Write it in a clear, concise manner, using simple language that anyone can understand. Think about a clear beginning, middle and end, and use verbs in active voice. This makes it easy to read and follow. A simple narrative of events makes it easy for your team to implement and test.

Alternative flows are equally important. These describe what happens when things don't go according to plan. What errors might occur? What user actions could cause unexpected outcomes? How does the system handle these scenarios? For example, what happens if the user enters invalid payment information, or if the network connection drops? This is where you would detail the system's responses to ensure graceful handling of problems. Thorough alternative flows are crucial for robust and reliable systems.

Exception handling is a crucial aspect of robust software design. Detailing how your system responds to different exception scenarios is critical for a complete use case description. This includes not only the technical aspects, such as error messages and logging, but also how the user experience is impacted. Consider user-friendly error messages and options for recovery, and ensure smooth integration with the overall user experience. A good description of error handling improves the overall usability.

Using clear and concise language is critical for effective communication. Avoid jargon, technical terms, or ambiguity. Focus on plain language that everyone can understand, ensuring every member of your Agile team understands the flow and requirements. Write as you would talk. This makes the description understandable to a wide audience, avoiding technical misunderstandings. This contributes to collaborative development.

The use case description is a living document. It should be revisited and updated throughout the development lifecycle, reflecting changes and refinements to the software. Keep it relevant to reflect the iterative nature of Agile development. Regular updates improve accuracy and maintain a shared understanding. This keeps the information fresh and consistent with the developing software. This ensures the use case description stays relevant to the current version.

3 Class Diagrams

Classes represent the building blocks of your object-oriented system. Think of them as blueprints for objects, defining their attributes (data they hold) and methods (actions they perform). For example, a Customer class might have attributes like name, address, and customerID, and methods such as placeOrder() and updateAddress(). Understanding this fundamental concept is crucial for effective class diagram creation. Precisely defining these elements ensures a clear and unambiguous representation of your system's structure. Careful consideration during this initial stage directly impacts the clarity and maintainability of your final software product. Properly defined classes and their attributes reduce the possibility of ambiguity and unnecessary modifications throughout the development lifecycle. This leads to more efficient coding and collaboration within development teams.

Relationships define how classes interact with each other. The most common types are association, aggregation, and composition. Association is a general relationship indicating a connection between two classes; for example, a Customer is associated with an Order. Aggregation represents a "has-a" relationship where one class contains another, but the contained class can exist independently; a Department might aggregate several Employees, but an employee can exist even without a department. Composition, a stronger form of aggregation, implies a "part-of" relationship where the contained class cannot exist independently of the containing class; for instance, an Engine is a part of a Car, and the engine cannot exist without the car. Choosing the correct type of relationship is critical to accurately modeling the system's dependencies and ensure the integrity of your object-oriented design. Inaccurate representation may lead to future code refactoring and potential implementation problems.

Inheritance, also known as generalization or specialization, allows you to create new classes (subclasses) based on existing classes (superclasses). Subclasses inherit the attributes and methods of their superclasses, adding their own specific features. This promotes code reusability and reduces redundancy. For instance, a PremiumCustomer class could inherit from the Customer class, adding attributes like discountPercentage and methods such as applyDiscount(). Inheritance helps you model hierarchical relationships effectively, simplifying complex structures and fostering a better understanding of class relationships within the system. This approach leads to enhanced code readability and maintainability, allowing future developers to easily grasp the system's intricacies.

Beyond the basics, advanced class modeling techniques enhance the expressiveness and precision of your diagrams. Abstract classes provide a blueprint for subclasses, defining common attributes and methods without creating instances. Interfaces specify a contract that classes must adhere to, ensuring consistent behavior. These tools allow you to create more flexible and extensible designs. Consider the case of an e-commerce platform. You might design an abstract class PaymentProcessor with methods like processPayment() and refundPayment(). Concrete classes like CreditCardPayment and PayPalPayment could inherit from this abstract class, offering concrete implementations for each payment type. The judicious use of abstract classes and interfaces allows for enhanced flexibility and maintainability of your code base.

Effective class diagram creation requires careful planning and a deep understanding of your system's structure. Begin by identifying the core entities and their attributes. Then, define the relationships between these entities, ensuring accuracy and consistency. Remember to use inheritance to model hierarchical relationships. Finally, utilize advanced techniques like abstract classes and interfaces to achieve greater flexibility. Regularly review and refine your diagrams as your understanding of the system evolves, ensuring your models remain accurate, relevant, and support clear communication between stakeholders. A well-structured class diagram, thoughtfully created, acts as a powerful tool for reducing ambiguity, guiding efficient development, and producing robust, adaptable software. This enhances not only the initial development process but also improves the long-term maintenance and scalability of your application. It promotes consistency and understanding within your development team, which is crucial for any project's success.

3.1 Classes and Attributes

Classes are the fundamental building blocks in object-oriented design, representing real-world entities or concepts within your software system. Think of them as blueprints for objects; each class defines a set of attributes (data) and methods (functions) that objects of that class will possess. For instance, a Customer class might have attributes like customerID, name, and address, and methods such as placeOrder() and updateAddress(). Understanding this foundational concept is crucial for creating well-structured and maintainable software. Effective class design involves careful consideration of responsibility and cohesion, ensuring that each class has a clear purpose and doesn't take on too much. This minimizes complexity and improves code reusability, a key principle in Agile development.

Attributes, on the other hand, are the characteristics or properties of a class. They represent the data associated with each object of that class. These attributes can be of various data types, such as integers, strings, booleans, or even other classes (leading to complex relationships we'll explore later). Consider our Customer class again; the customerID would likely be an integer, the name a string, and the address might be another class entirely, perhaps containing attributes like street, city, and zip code. Choosing appropriate data types is essential for data integrity and efficiency. For example, using an integer for a customer ID ensures that only numerical values are used, preventing errors caused by unexpected input. The careful selection of attributes directly impacts the quality and effectiveness of your software.

Let's delve into how to effectively define attributes within your UML class diagrams. The notation is straightforward: within the class rectangle, you list the attributes, typically along with their data types. For instance, you might represent the Customer class's attributes as follows: customerID: int, name: String, address: Address. This simple yet powerful representation allows for clear communication among team members, ensuring everyone understands the structure of the data. Consistent and clear notation is key to maintaining a shared understanding of the design within the Agile process, making collaboration more effective. Remember, consistent UML notation reduces ambiguity and aids team comprehension, ensuring everyone is on the same page when it comes to the software's underlying structure.

Visibility modifiers are another important aspect of attribute definition. These modifiers, often represented by symbols such as + (public), - (private), and # (protected), specify the accessibility of attributes from other classes. Public attributes are accessible from anywhere, private attributes are only accessible within the class itself, and protected attributes are accessible within the class and its subclasses. Choosing the appropriate visibility is critical for encapsulation, a fundamental principle of object-oriented design. Encapsulation protects the internal state of an object, preventing unintended modifications and improving the robustness of your software. This practice promotes cleaner code, reduces dependencies, and simplifies maintenance. In an Agile environment, where changes are frequent, such practices are crucial.

The correct use of attributes is vital for a successful project. Overly complex attributes can lead to unnecessary complexity and hinder the efficiency of your code. Conversely, insufficient attributes can lead to missing or inaccurate data representation, potentially impacting system functionality. You need to strike a balance. Avoid redundant or unnecessary attributes, aiming for a concise yet comprehensive representation of the object's essential characteristics. It's better to refactor and add more if needed than to start with unnecessarily complex attributes. During the iterative process of Agile development, this allows for flexibility and adaptability as requirements evolve. Remember that well-defined attributes significantly improve data integrity and the overall efficiency of your software system.

Consider the potential impact of attribute changes on the overall design. Modifying an attribute's data type or adding a new attribute might require changes in other parts of the system. Therefore, careful planning and consideration are necessary to minimize the ripple effects of such changes, especially important within the iterative framework of Agile development. Thorough testing and validation are essential to ensure that changes don't introduce bugs or inconsistencies into the system. This rigorous approach safeguards the integrity of your software and reduces development risks.

To reiterate, mastering classes and attributes is paramount to building robust, maintainable software using UML within an Agile context. By understanding how to define classes, choose appropriate attributes, and utilize visibility modifiers effectively, you lay the foundation for a well-structured and scalable software solution. Remember, clear communication through consistent UML notation is crucial for successful collaboration within your Agile team. This careful attention to detail ensures that the software design reflects the requirements and adapts effectively to evolving needs. The key takeaway is to strive for simplicity and clarity in your class and attribute definitions, focusing on functionality and maintainability throughout the design process. The benefits are well worth the effort.

3.2 Relationships

Relationships in class diagrams are the glue that holds your object-oriented design together. Understanding how to model them effectively is crucial for building robust and maintainable software. Think of them as the connections, the interactions, defining how different parts of your system communicate and collaborate. Without accurate relationship modeling, your diagrams become a disorganized mess, hindering comprehension and leading to design flaws.

Several types of relationships exist, each with its own unique characteristics and implications. The most fundamental is the association, representing a general connection between two classes. For instance, a Customer might be associated with multiple Orders, indicating a customer can place many orders, and each order belongs to a single customer. This is a straightforward relationship, yet vital to capturing the essential dynamics between entities. Defining the multiplicity (e.g., one-to-many, many-to-many) clarifies the nature of the connection and its potential ramifications.

Inheritance, or generalization, signifies a "is-a" relationship. Consider a scenario with Animal, Dog, and Cat classes. Dog and Cat inherit from Animal, inheriting common attributes like name and age, but also defining their unique characteristics. This promotes code reusability and reduces redundancy, resulting in a cleaner, more maintainable design. Properly implementing inheritance requires careful consideration of the hierarchical structure, ensuring a consistent and logical representation of the relationships involved.

Aggregation and composition represent different forms of "whole-part" relationships. Aggregation indicates a weaker connection; the parts can exist independently of the whole. For example, a Department might aggregate several Employees. The employees can exist even if the department is dissolved. Composition, on the other hand, denotes a stronger relationship; the parts cannot exist without the whole. For example, a Car is composed of an Engine, Wheels, and other components. These components cannot exist independently of the car. Distinguishing between aggregation and composition is critical for understanding the lifespan and dependencies within your system.

Navigability defines the direction of access between classes. A unidirectional association allows access from one class to another but not vice-versa. For instance, an Order might know its associated Customer, but the Customer may not directly access its related Orders. Bidirectional associations allow access in both directions, providing a more complete representation of the relationship. Choosing the correct navigation depends on the specific needs of your design, balancing detail with simplicity. Overly complex navigation schemes can lead to unnecessary complexity and make the diagram difficult to understand.

The importance of carefully defining these relationships cannot be overstated. Incorrectly modeling relationships will lead to inaccurate representations of your system, making it difficult for your team to grasp the overall design and implement it correctly. This might lead to bugs and inconsistencies that are extremely costly to fix later in the development process. Thorough relationship modeling is an investment in the clarity, robustness, and maintainability of your software. A well-defined relationship model simplifies communication, streamlines development, and ultimately contributes to the success of your project.

Remember that the choice of which relationship to use often depends on the specific context of your model. Careful consideration of the relationships between your classes, including the multiplicity, navigability, and the strength of the connection, will result in a more accurate and maintainable UML model. This accurate modeling is crucial in facilitating clear communication and collaboration within your agile team. Using precise and well-defined relationships within your class diagrams is a key factor in the success of your agile software development project. This will lead to a more accurate representation of the system, making it easier to develop, maintain and update the software. A clear, well-structured model is your best ally when facing complex development challenges. The time invested in crafting precise and accurate relationships will greatly outweigh the costs incurred by fixing issues caused by poorly defined relationships. This will reduce the time spent debugging and testing and improve the overall quality of the final product. Ultimately, taking care to model these relationships properly will make all other steps in the software development process much smoother.

3.3 Inheritance

Inheritance, in the context of UML class diagrams, is a powerful mechanism for creating reusable and maintainable software designs. It allows you to define a general class, called a superclass or parent class, and then create specialized classes, called subclasses or child classes, that inherit the properties and behaviors of the superclass. This promotes code reuse, reducing redundancy and enhancing the overall efficiency of your development process. Think of it like building upon a foundation – you don't need to reinvent the wheel each time you want to create a new, similar object.

Consider a simple example: you might have a superclass called "Animal" with attributes like "name" and "age," and methods like "eat" and "sleep." Subclasses like "Dog," "Cat," and "Bird" would inherit these attributes and methods, but they could also have their own unique attributes (like "breed" for "Dog") and methods (like "bark" for "Dog"). This structured approach simplifies the modeling process, improving readability and understandability across your entire project. The inheritance relationship clearly establishes a hierarchy, making the relationships between the classes explicitly defined. Careful consideration of these relationships forms the foundation for a scalable and robust system.

The beauty of inheritance lies in its ability to extend functionality without rewriting existing code. If you need to add a new method to the "Animal" superclass, that method automatically becomes available to all subclasses, saving you a great deal of effort. This is especially useful when dealing with complex software systems where maintaining consistency and managing changes across many classes becomes critical. Imagine needing to update a core functionality in numerous classes independently. With inheritance, you only need to update the parent class, which then trickles down to all its children classes automatically.

However, inheritance should be used judiciously. Overuse can lead to tightly coupled code, making it difficult to change or maintain. Consider the "is-a" relationship when deciding whether to use inheritance. A subclass should truly be a specialized type of the superclass. If the relationship is more of a "has-a" relationship, consider using composition instead. This ensures each class maintains its own independence while working together within the project. This approach promotes flexibility and maintainability and reduces the likelihood of unwanted consequences.

Furthermore, understanding different types of inheritance is vital for effective implementation. Single inheritance, where a subclass inherits from only one superclass, is simpler to manage but limits flexibility. Multiple inheritance, where a subclass can inherit from multiple superclasses, offers more flexibility but can introduce complexity in resolving conflicts if superclasses have methods with the same name. Choosing the appropriate type depends entirely on the specific design requirements of your project. Poorly chosen inheritance models can lead to complex, less manageable and harder-to-maintain code bases. Understanding the implications of each type of inheritance is paramount.

Effective use of inheritance involves careful planning and design. Start by identifying the commonalities among your classes and group them together into a superclass. Then, define subclasses that inherit the common attributes and methods while adding their own unique characteristics. This approach ensures a clean and organized class structure, simplifying maintenance and promoting code reuse. Remember to regularly review and refine your inheritance structure as your project evolves, adapting your design to new requirements and potential improvements. Remember, the goal of using inheritance is to create a well-structured and maintainable software system. It's a valuable tool, but it's essential to use it appropriately. By thoughtfully implementing inheritance and being mindful of its potential downsides, you can unlock its considerable power to streamline your development process and build a robust and scalable application. Don't be afraid to refactor your inheritance structure if you find it becoming too complex or unwieldy. A well-designed inheritance structure improves clarity and simplifies the entire development cycle.

Finally, consider the use of abstract classes and interfaces. Abstract classes define a common interface for subclasses but may also contain some implemented methods. Interfaces, on the other hand, only define a common interface without any implementation. Using abstract classes and interfaces enables even greater flexibility and maintainability. These allow you to define a clear structure and common behavior without dictating the precise implementation in each subclass. This loose coupling adds to the robustness and extensibility of the overall design. The result is a more flexible and more adaptive architecture suited to change, a key consideration in the agile enterprise. Careful use of abstract classes and interfaces complements and enhances the power of inheritance.

3.4 Aggregation and Composition

Aggregation represents a "has-a" relationship where one class contains instances of another class, but the contained class can exist independently. Think of a car and its wheels: the car has wheels, but the wheels can exist separately from the car. This relationship is less tightly coupled than composition. For example, a university has students, but the students exist independently of the university. They can attend other universities, or even not attend any. This is a clear example of aggregation, because the lifecycle of one entity does not directly depend on the other. The removal of a student from the university's system doesn't remove the student from existence. This distinction is crucial when designing your class diagrams and thinking about how you want to represent the relationships within your system.

Consider a library system. A library has books; a book can exist even if it's not currently part of a library's collection. The book has its own existence, independent of any library. You could represent this relationship in your UML class diagram with an open diamond on the Library class side indicating the aggregation relationship. This illustrates that the library doesn't own or control the life cycle of the books; the books exist independently. The choice to use aggregation versus composition needs careful consideration. This ensures the most accurate representation of the relationship in your model.

Composition, on the other hand, denotes a stronger "part-of" relationship. Here, the contained class cannot exist independently of the containing class. Imagine a house and its rooms; a room cannot exist without a house. This is a highly coupled relationship. Similarly, a company's departments are composed within the company itself; when the company ceases to exist, so do its departments. In this scenario, the destruction or removal of the parent class (the company) directly affects the lifecycle of the child class (the departments). Therefore, the composition relationship needs to reflect this inherent dependency to ensure your model accurately represents the relationships within the system.

Let's delve into a more complex example: an order management system. An order has order items, but the order items are intimately linked to the order itself—they don't make sense outside the context of that specific order. If an order is canceled, so too are its associated items. They cannot exist separately. This is a prime example of composition; a filled diamond on the Order class side of the relationship in your UML diagram clearly displays this strong dependency. This helps developers understand the interconnectedness of components within your system. This detail in your class diagram avoids ambiguity and ensures your team understands the implied dependencies.

The difference between aggregation and composition is subtle but critically important for accurately representing your system's structure in UML. Misrepresenting these relationships could lead to inconsistencies and errors in your design. Think carefully about the lifecycle dependencies between your classes. Can the parts exist independently of the whole? If not, then use composition. If they can exist separately, then aggregation is a more appropriate choice. The accurate portrayal of the relationship is not a minor detail in the design process; it's a critical step that affects the system's design and consistency.

Choosing the correct relationship type influences not only the UML diagram's accuracy but also the underlying code structure. If you model a relationship as aggregation when it's actually composition, your code might become overly complex or even function incorrectly. For instance, you might accidentally delete only the 'parent' class, leaving orphaned 'child' objects. This problem could cause data inconsistencies. Conversely, modeling a composition relationship as aggregation might make managing the whole and its parts less efficient in the code. Careful consideration of the type of relationship enhances the efficiency and maintainability of your software.

Therefore, meticulous attention to detail in your UML diagrams is paramount. Not only does it improve the clarity and understanding of your design, but it also directly impacts the efficiency and maintainability of your software development process. A well-defined UML model serves as a powerful communication tool, facilitating seamless collaboration amongst team members, and guiding the development process. By focusing on the intricacies of relationships like aggregation and composition, you build a robust foundation for your project. Clear modeling techniques, like the proper application of aggregation and composition, contribute significantly to producing well-structured and efficient software applications. Remember, a well-defined UML model serves as a blueprint for your application, thus any errors in representation directly impact the development outcome. Mastering these seemingly simple concepts will help you become a more effective software engineer.

3.5 Advanced Class Modeling

Designing robust and scalable systems requires a deep understanding of advanced class modeling techniques. Beyond the basics of classes, attributes, and relationships, we need to explore concepts like abstract classes, interfaces, and advanced relationship types to create truly flexible and maintainable designs. Consider the challenge of modeling a complex e-commerce system: a simple class diagram might suffice initially, but as requirements evolve, a more sophisticated approach becomes essential.

Abstract classes provide a blueprint for subclasses, defining common attributes and methods while preventing direct instantiation. Think of an abstract "Product" class, specifying attributes like "name" and "price," but leaving the implementation of specific product details to subclasses such as "Book," "Electronics," or "Clothing." This promotes code reusability and reduces redundancy, making future expansion and maintenance significantly simpler. This structured approach avoids the pitfalls of repetitive code and allows for easier management of system evolution.

Interfaces define a contract that classes must adhere to, specifying a set of methods without providing implementation details. For our e-commerce example, an "Orderable" interface could define methods like "addToCart" and "removeFromCart," which any product class can implement, ensuring consistent interaction regardless of the product type. This promotes loose coupling, making the system more resilient to changes and allowing for greater flexibility in adding new product types or features. In effect, using interfaces improves the overall design by enforcing consistency, improving maintainability and reducing the impact of alterations.

Moving beyond basic associations, consider the nuances of aggregation and composition. Aggregation represents a "has-a" relationship where one class contains another, but the contained class can exist independently. For instance, an "Order" class might aggregate multiple "Product" classes, as an order can exist even if some products are removed. However, composition represents a stronger "part-of" relationship where the contained class cannot exist without the containing class. A "Car" class might compose of "Engine" and "Wheels" classes; an engine can't exist independently of a car. Careful distinction between these relationship types clarifies the structural integrity of your system, greatly enhancing its design quality.

Generalization, commonly known as inheritance, allows classes to inherit attributes and methods from parent classes, forming a hierarchical structure. In our e-commerce system, a "Customer" class might inherit from a more general "User" class, inheriting common attributes like "name" and "email," reducing redundancy. However, careful consideration of inheritance is crucial to avoid problems such as tight coupling and the potential for fragile base classes. Overuse of inheritance can create tightly coupled and difficult-to-maintain systems, negatively impacting development. Strategic and thoughtful use of inheritance improves your code's flexibility and facilitates easier modification.

Advanced class modeling often involves incorporating constraints and stereotypes. Constraints specify rules that must be satisfied by the system, such as cardinality limitations on relationships (e.g., a customer can have many orders, but an order can only belong to one customer), or data type restrictions on attributes. Stereotypes are used to further clarify the nature of classes or relationships by using UML notation to specify roles or purposes of system components; for example, identifying an interface with a <> stereotype. Well-defined constraints and stereotypes improve model clarity and understanding, crucial for effective communication within a development team. Clarity greatly reduces ambiguity and improves the efficiency of collaboration and maintenance.

The strategic use of these advanced class modeling techniques elevates your design from a simple representation of system components to a robust model reflecting the system's complexities and future adaptability. This isn't merely about generating diagrams; it's about building a foundation for a scalable, maintainable, and highly adaptable software system. The effort spent mastering these techniques provides a significant return in efficiency and reliability throughout the entire software development lifecycle. Through careful application of these tools and practices, one can navigate the complexities of software development with confidence and efficiency. The ultimate result: a software solution better equipped to meet current and future demands.

4 Sequence Diagrams

Sequence diagrams offer a powerful way to visualize the interactions between objects in a system, revealing the dynamic flow of messages and methods calls over time. They are indispensable for understanding complex behavior and identifying potential bottlenecks or issues early in the development process, significantly improving the efficiency and clarity of your design. Using them effectively will help you to achieve more robust and well-structured software.

Consider a simple e-commerce application. A customer wants to purchase an item. The sequence diagram would show the interaction between the customer (actor), the shopping cart object, the product catalog object, the payment gateway object, and the order processing object. Each object has its lifeline represented as a vertical line showing its existence throughout the interaction. The messages passed between objects are shown as arrows, clarifying how the purchase progresses step-by-step. This visualization helps you understand the dependencies between these various components and anticipates challenges in integration, especially before a single line of code is written.

The most crucial element in constructing effective sequence diagrams is understanding the concept of "lifelines." These vertical lines represent the existence of objects during the interaction. Each lifeline starts when the object is created and ends when it is destroyed. The placement of lifelines on the diagram is critical; objects that interact more closely are typically placed closer together, visually reflecting their strong relationship. Proper arrangement significantly increases the readability and usability of your diagrams. The clarity of a well-made sequence diagram cannot be overstated.

Messages are depicted as arrows connecting the lifelines, representing communication between objects. These messages can be synchronous (blocking), where the caller waits for a response before continuing, or asynchronous (non-blocking), where the caller continues its execution without waiting. Different arrow styles can further clarify the type of message, such as solid arrows for synchronous calls and dashed arrows for asynchronous calls. Accurate depiction of message types is crucial for understanding the system's responsiveness and timing. You might be surprised at the clarity this provides to your code design and testing processes.

Creating a sequence diagram begins with identifying the key objects involved in the interaction. This involves careful consideration of your class diagram and a deep understanding of your system's requirements. Once you've identified these objects, you can start drawing their lifelines. Next, you need to determine the order in which the objects interact and the messages exchanged between them. Remember that a well-structured sequence diagram should clearly show the flow of control and data through the system. This involves determining the start and end points for each message and the specific parameters passed with each message, further enhancing the accuracy and completeness of your representation.

Remember, while details are important, clarity should always take precedence. A cluttered and confusing diagram is worse than none at all. Avoid unnecessary detail; instead, focus on the critical interactions that demonstrate the core functionality. Employ appropriate levels of abstraction to avoid overwhelming the reader. A clear diagram easily communicates the desired information without overwhelming the viewer with extraneous detail. You should always aim for a balance between comprehensive information and efficient communication in all your design documentation. After all, this is intended to streamline the development process, and a complex diagram will only impede that goal.

Focus on creating diagrams that are easily understandable and maintainable, prioritizing a balance between detail and clarity to enhance collaboration and communication amongst the entire team. Always keep in mind the goal: a clearer understanding of the system's behavior, which will lead to more efficient development, and less debugging later on. Regularly review and update your sequence diagrams as your design evolves. Incorporating feedback and changes will maintain the accuracy of your documentation, while fostering collaboration within your team.

This ensures your documentation remains an invaluable asset throughout the entire development lifecycle. Consistent review and refinement is key to its long term usefulness.

In the context of agile development, sequence diagrams play a vital role in iterative design and rapid prototyping. They allow the team to quickly visualize the interactions of objects and components, identifying potential conflicts or areas needing improvement. This visual tool aids in collaborative brainstorming sessions, facilitating a shared understanding of the system's dynamic behavior before committing to large blocks of code. Regularly revisiting and updating these diagrams in each iteration allows the design to adapt easily to evolving requirements and emerging issues. By using sequence diagrams this way, you make it considerably simpler to stay abreast of ongoing modifications to the system's design. Remember this flexibility is a cornerstone of agile methodology.

4.1 Message Flows

Sequence diagrams offer a powerful way to visualize the interactions between objects within your system. They're not just static representations; instead, they capture the dynamic flow of messages, showing how different parts of your application work together over time. Understanding this dynamic flow is key to building robust and efficient software. Think of it like a play script for your objects, outlining their dialogue and actions. Each object has a role, and the messages are their lines.

Let's delve into the specifics. The fundamental building block of a sequence diagram is the lifeline, which represents the existence of an object throughout the interaction. You'll see these depicted as vertical lines, with the object's name at the top. Messages, represented by arrows, show the communication between these lifelines. A solid arrow indicates a synchronous message – the sender waits for a response from the receiver. A dashed arrow represents an asynchronous message – the sender doesn't wait for an immediate reply. This distinction is crucial for understanding the timing and flow of your application. Consider, for example, a simple e-commerce system where a customer places an order. The sequence diagram will showcase the interactions between the customer, the order processing system, the inventory management system, and the payment gateway. You'll clearly see how the "place order" message triggers a cascade of messages, each with its specific role in fulfilling the order.

Now, let's talk about message flows. These aren't just random exchanges; they follow a structured path, driven by the logic of your application. Think carefully about the order of messages, as this directly reflects the sequence of operations in your system. A well-structured message flow ensures a smooth and predictable execution. A poorly structured one, however, can lead to errors, deadlocks, or unexpected behavior. For instance, an incorrect message sequence in the e-commerce example could result in an order being processed before the payment is confirmed, leading to potential financial issues. A key aspect of designing effective message flows is managing dependencies. Certain messages might need to occur before others. Properly representing these dependencies in your diagram is vital for understanding the system's behavior. Creating clear and concise sequence diagrams requires careful planning. Start by identifying the key objects involved in the interaction. Next, determine the sequence of messages exchanged between these objects. Pay attention to the timing and type of each message (synchronous or asynchronous). Once you've established the flow, represent it visually using the lifeline and message notations. Remember, the goal is to create a diagram that's easy to understand and interpret. Avoid unnecessary complexity by focusing on the essential interactions. Using clear and consistent naming conventions for your objects and messages enhances readability and aids in collaboration among team members.

Remember, sequence diagrams are a living document. As your understanding of the system evolves, your diagram should reflect those changes. Regularly review and update your diagrams to ensure they accurately represent the current state of your application. Use them as a collaborative tool, discussing them with your team to identify potential issues or areas for improvement. It's a powerful tool for proactive problem-solving. Think of it as a form of preventative maintenance, identifying potential issues before they become major problems. Effective use of sequence diagrams improves the overall design and reduces the likelihood of bugs. The practice leads to cleaner, more efficient code, saving time and resources throughout the development process. Through careful design and iterative refinement, your sequence diagrams will become an indispensable part of your Agile development workflow. They're not just diagrams; they're a communication tool, a design tool, and ultimately a vital component in building high-quality software.

4.2 Lifelines

Lifelines represent the existence of an object over time within a sequence diagram. Think of them as vertical lines, each representing a specific object participating in the interaction. They visually track an object's life, from its creation to its eventual destruction or the end of the scenario being modeled. Understanding lifelines is crucial for properly illustrating object interactions and identifying potential concurrency issues. Their simplicity belies their importance in clarifying complex interactions. Proper use ensures the sequence diagram effectively communicates the desired behavior.

A lifeline begins with a small rectangle, often representing the object's creation. This rectangle might be labeled with the object's name or class, providing context to the lifeline. The lifeline extends vertically downwards, indicating the object's continued existence. Messages sent to and received by the object are denoted by arrows connected to the lifeline. These arrows show the flow of information and collaboration among objects. Note that the lifeline itself isn't just a visual aid; it holds implicit meaning, reflecting the object's state and its role in the interaction. A missing lifeline can lead to misunderstandings in the interaction sequence, obscuring crucial information.

Messages between objects are represented by arrows connecting their respective lifelines. A solid arrowhead signifies a synchronous message—the sender pauses until the receiver responds. A dashed arrowhead indicates an asynchronous message—the sender doesn't wait for an immediate reply. The message itself usually contains a brief description of the action or information being exchanged. Clearly identifying message types is crucial. A missing or improperly classified message can radically change the interpreted sequence of events, leading to incorrect conclusions about the system's behavior. Pay close attention to the detail of each message; precision here is vital for effective communication.

Consider, for example, a simple online banking system. You, the user (represented by a lifeline), initiate a transaction by sending a message to the banking system's object. The system then interacts with a database object, retrieving account information through an asynchronous message. The account object might communicate with an authentication object to verify your credentials. These interactions create a chain of events, all visually represented along their lifelines. The lifelines clearly display the flow of control and data, showing how each component contributes to the entire transaction. Without the lifelines, the relationships would be significantly more difficult to understand.

Focus on accurately depicting the object's life cycle and involvement in the overall process. Incorrectly placing messages or omitting crucial interactions can lead to misinterpreted scenarios and potential errors. The lifeline's length, although seemingly simple, can itself contain information. An abnormally short lifeline suggests the object might play a less significant role than initially conceived. A long one could highlight an object that requires refactoring due to potentially excessive responsibilities. Careful examination of lifeline length, and its contextual implication, offers the UML modeler invaluable insights into the system's architecture and design.

The placement of activation bars along the lifeline further refines its representation. Activation bars are rectangular boxes extending from the lifeline, indicating when the object is active (executing a method or action). These bars clearly show the periods when an object is actively engaged in processing. The absence or incorrect representation of activation bars can easily lead to a misleading illustration of an object's activity. Accurate placement is crucial for illustrating the flow of control and determining potential concurrency issues. Remember, an accurate sequence diagram needs to accurately reflect the system's functional specifications.

Furthermore, consider using destruction markers to indicate when an object is no longer needed. A destruction marker, usually an "X" at the end of a lifeline, signifies the object's termination. This clarifies the object's lifespan within the sequence. Omitting the destruction marker, particularly in scenarios where objects are explicitly destroyed, might obscure this crucial aspect of the object's life cycle and confuse interpretations of the sequence diagram. The omission of simple, yet powerful, visual cues like the destruction marker can create confusion and complicate the understanding of the system's behavior.

Finally, remember that sequence diagrams and lifelines are tools for communication and collaboration. While the details are important, remember that the ultimate goal is to make your design clear and easily understood by other members of your team. Clearly labeled lifelines, well-defined messages, and accurately placed activation bars and destruction markers are essential for conveying your intent and facilitating a smooth collaborative development process. Aim for clarity; an easily understandable diagram is more valuable than an overly complex one. Effective communication is paramount in the agile development process.

5 State Machine Diagrams

State machine diagrams offer a powerful way to visualize and understand the behavior of objects in a system. They're particularly useful when dealing with objects that change their behavior based on internal states and external events. Imagine a simple traffic light; its behavior—showing red, then green, then yellow—can be elegantly represented using a state machine. Each color represents a state, and the transitions between colors are triggered by events like a timer expiring or a sensor detecting a car.

These diagrams aren't just for simple examples, however. They're crucial for modeling complex systems where multiple states and transitions need clear articulation. Consider a software component responsible for handling network connections. It might have states like "connecting," "connected," "disconnected," and "error." Each transition between these states would be triggered by specific events, such as a successful connection attempt, a network failure, or a user's request to disconnect. The actions performed within these transitions might involve sending messages, updating internal data, or logging events.

Modeling these behaviors helps in clarifying the interactions between system components. It helps identify potential issues, and enables developers to predict how the system will react to various events. For instance, if the network connection component encounters an error, a well-defined state machine would specify the actions to take – perhaps retrying the connection, notifying the user, or activating a fail-safe mechanism. This level of detail prevents unexpected behavior and makes the software far more robust.

Let's delve into the core components of a state machine diagram. The most fundamental element is, of course, the state. A state represents a specific condition of the object at a particular time. It's characterized by the values of its attributes and its readiness to respond to incoming events. Then, you have the transitions, represented by arrows connecting states. These transitions are triggered by events, which are external stimuli or internal signals that cause the object to change from one state to another. Each transition can also involve an action, which is a task or operation performed during the transition.

Beyond the basics, state machine diagrams can incorporate several advanced features. Hierarchical state machines, for example, allow you to decompose complex states into smaller, more manageable sub-states. This structure improves readability and simplifies the design of complex systems. Another valuable feature is the concept of nested states, where a state can contain other states, creating a hierarchy that effectively models complex behaviors. Such nesting mirrors the way many real-world systems operate with layers of sub-systems interacting and changing state.

Consider an example of a more complex system: an automated teller machine (ATM). The ATM has various states like "idle," "card inserted," "PIN entered," "transaction in progress," and "transaction complete." Transitions between these states are triggered by events like inserting a card, entering a PIN, selecting a transaction type, or withdrawing cash. Actions performed during these transitions might involve reading the card, verifying the PIN, updating the account balance, and dispensing cash. A state machine diagram visually organizes all these states, transitions, events, and actions, creating a clear and concise model of the ATM's behavior.

You can use state machine diagrams to design and verify the behavior of your software components. By identifying all the states, transitions, events, and actions, you can create a comprehensive model of your system's behavior. It's a practice that yields valuable insights into the interactions within your system, leading to improved reliability and maintainability. Remember, thorough planning and well-defined states are critical. In short, state machine diagrams provide a systematic approach to designing and understanding complex software, enhancing communication and reducing errors. By focusing on precise descriptions of each component, you make the design much clearer, easier to maintain, and ultimately more reliable. The clarity offered by the diagrams translates directly to reduced development time and fewer bugs down the line. Employing these diagrams is not just a best practice, it's a critical tool for building high-quality, scalable software systems. You won't regret incorporating this powerful design tool into your agile development workflow. They are an essential part of the UML toolkit, particularly useful when dealing with systems that exhibit intricate state-dependent behaviors.

5.1 States and Transitions

Understanding state machine diagrams requires grasping the core concepts of states and transitions. A state represents a specific condition or situation an object can be in; think of it as a snapshot of the object at a particular moment in its lifecycle. For example, an order in an e-commerce system might have states like "placed," "processing," "shipped," and "delivered." Each of these represents a distinct phase in the order's journey. Transitions, conversely, are the dynamic actions that move an object from one state to another. They are triggered by events, such as a customer clicking the "place order" button, the warehouse receiving the order, or the delivery service confirming the shipment.

Now let's consider the practical application of this in UML. To model these states and transitions effectively, you need to use a standardized notation within your state machine diagrams. Each state is typically represented by a rounded rectangle containing the state's name. Transitions are depicted by arrows connecting these rectangles, labeled with the event that triggers the transition. For instance, you might have a transition arrow from the "placed" state to the "processing" state, labeled with the event "order received." This clearly illustrates the flow between different stages of the order. The simplicity of this visual representation facilitates easy understanding and collaboration among developers and stakeholders.

Beyond the basic representation, UML state machine diagrams allow for more detailed modeling, adding layers of complexity. One such enhancement involves including actions within the transitions. These actions, performed during the transition, are often vital. Consider a scenario where the transition from "order placed" to "processing" involves updating the database to reflect the change in the order's status. This critical action, performed during the transition, isn't just about moving between states; it's about the system reacting and updating its data accordingly. This is where the power of UML's detailed representation truly shines, enabling a more comprehensive understanding of not just the state changes but the associated system actions.

Further refinement is possible through the introduction of guards and activities. A guard is a condition that must be met for a transition to occur; only if the guard evaluates to true will the transition proceed. Imagine adding a payment verification guard to the transition from "placed" to "processing"; the transition wouldn't proceed unless the payment is verified. Activities, on the other hand, represent behaviors that occur within a state. For example, the "processing" state might involve an activity indicating that the order is being assembled for shipping. Thus, guards add conditions for transitions, and activities enhance descriptions within individual states, resulting in a highly nuanced state machine model.

These advanced concepts contribute to the overall precision of UML state machine diagrams. This precision reduces ambiguity and strengthens the alignment between model and code, leading to less rework and a smoother development process. Incorporating guards and activities allows you to effectively model real-world complexities, ensuring that your diagrams accurately capture the subtle nuances within the system's behavior. A well-constructed state machine diagram, therefore, isn't merely a visual representation but a powerful tool that aids in creating a robust and accurate model of a system's dynamic behavior, contributing significantly to the agile methodology. It is a crucial element for efficient and successful software development, minimizing potential flaws before they manifest in the completed product.

When applying this in the context of your agile development process, remember that state machine diagrams, like other UML diagrams, are iterative tools. They should evolve alongside the project, reflecting changes and refinements in the system's design. Don't strive for absolute perfection on your first attempt; it's about using the tool to clarify understanding, communicate effectively with your team, and to avoid later issues. Start with simple diagrams, focusing on the core states and transitions, and then progressively add more details as needed. This incremental approach is critical in the agile methodology, ensuring your model stays aligned with the ever-evolving nature of agile development. The iterative approach ensures your diagrams remain useful throughout the project's lifecycle.

Finally, consider the value of collaboration when creating and using state machine diagrams. Involve relevant stakeholders, such as developers, testers, and business analysts, in the process. Encourage feedback and review sessions to ensure everyone has a shared understanding of the system's behavior. Remember, a successful UML model, regardless of type, is a collaborative product, ensuring everyone's insight contributes to a more robust and accurate representation. This collaborative effort not only improves the accuracy of the state machine diagram but also promotes a stronger understanding of the project requirements. This shared understanding minimizes misinterpretations and avoids costly rework later in the development process, significantly contributing to the overall efficiency and success of the project. Remember, the goal isn't just a perfect diagram, but a shared understanding that accelerates the entire software development process.

5.2 Events and Actions

Events and actions are fundamental building blocks in state machine diagrams. They represent the triggers and responses that drive the behavior of objects within a system. Understanding how to model these effectively is critical for creating accurate and robust state machine diagrams, crucial for visualizing complex system behavior and streamlining the development process. Accurate modeling reduces ambiguity and enables efficient collaboration among team members, enhancing the overall development process significantly.

An event is simply something that happens, a signal or occurrence that can alter the state of an object. This could be a user clicking a button, a timer expiring, or a message received from another object. We model these events using descriptive names clearly conveying their purpose and context within the system. This clarity is essential for maintainability and understanding, especially in large and complex systems. Consider using a naming convention that reflects the system's domain terminology. For example, instead of a generic "buttonClick," use "submitOrder" if that is the specific context. This level of detail ensures everyone working on the project shares a consistent understanding.

Actions, on the other hand, are the responses to events. When an event occurs, an action is performed. These can be simple operations, like updating a variable, or more complex processes, such as calling another method or sending a message to another object. The key is to define actions precisely, detailing exactly what happens when an event triggers them. Ambiguity in defining actions can lead to unforeseen errors and difficulties during implementation. Actions should be concisely documented to ensure consistency and prevent future misunderstandings. Consider using pseudo-code or a similar structured approach to clarify any complex actions.

Consider a simple example: a traffic light. The events are "timer expires," "sensor detects vehicle," and "manual override." The actions associated with these events might include changing the light color, activating a buzzer, or adjusting the timer. This simple model illustrates how events trigger actions, which in turn dictate the flow and overall behavior of the system. Using clear, concise terms is paramount; the consistency ensures the functionality of the model aligns seamlessly with the eventual software implementation.

It's vital to remember that events and actions are intrinsically linked. An event acts as the stimulus, initiating the performance of an action. This cause-and-effect relationship dictates the flow of the state machine, guiding the system through its various states based on the events triggered and subsequent actions performed. To avoid complexity, keep events and actions appropriately granular. Avoid overly encompassing actions or events that cover multiple functional aspects. Small, manageable units increase maintainability and ease of comprehension.

Defining these events and actions requires careful consideration of the system's requirements and behavior. A well-defined set of events and actions makes the resulting state machine more understandable, maintainable, and easier to debug. This ultimately leads to more efficient development cycles, translating into reduced project timelines and a more robust end product. Use cases are often invaluable here. Refer to your previously crafted use case diagrams to define events and actions that directly correspond to the users' interactions with the system. The result is a more seamless and intuitive user experience.

The relationship between events and actions is not always one-to-one. A single event might trigger multiple actions, or several events might trigger a single action. It's crucial to carefully model these relationships, ensuring the state machine accurately represents the system's complexity. This meticulous approach is essential for creating accurate state machine diagrams. These diagrams will help you and your development team thoroughly understand the interactions between various system components.

Remember that the precision of these diagrams is directly reflected in the quality and efficiency of your development process. Clear diagrams prevent ambiguities, saving time and avoiding costly errors during implementation. The clarity enhances team communication and fosters smoother collaboration among developers. Thoroughly documenting events and actions enhances collaboration among team members, leading to more efficient and error-free development cycles. A clear and understandable state machine diagram, with precisely defined events and actions, becomes a vital asset to developers during implementation and maintenance.

Effective modeling of events and actions requires meticulous planning and consideration of all possible system interactions. By carefully identifying potential events and defining corresponding actions, you create a robust and resilient state machine diagram, enhancing the predictability and reliability of your system. This translates to a high-quality product, reducing the risks associated with unforeseen behavior or errors.

Employing a collaborative approach, with frequent reviews and revisions, ensures that the models are accurate and reflect the actual system requirements efficiently. Consider incorporating iterative modeling techniques, continuously refining your diagrams as new information becomes available, ensuring a seamless transition between the design and implementation phases. Remember to consistently review and refine your model throughout the development lifecycle. This iterative approach to modeling will allow for flexibility and adaptation to changing requirements.

5.3 Advanced State Modeling

Advanced state modeling elevates your understanding of state machine diagrams beyond the basics. We're moving past simple state transitions to incorporate powerful concepts that significantly improve the clarity, maintainability, and expressiveness of your models. This allows for a more accurate representation of complex system behaviors, leading to more robust and less error-prone software.

Consider, for instance, the scenario of designing a sophisticated vending machine. A simple state machine might show states like "Idle," "Selecting Item," "Dispensing Item," and "Returning Change." However, a real-world vending machine possesses far more intricate behavior. It needs to handle situations like credit card failures, insufficient funds, item jams, and even network connectivity issues—none of which are easily represented using only basic states and transitions. Advanced techniques are essential for handling such complexity.

Nested states provide an elegant solution. Instead of a monolithic "Dispensing Item" state, you might nest multiple sub-states within it. This could include "Initiating Dispensing," "Dispensing Item," "Verifying Dispensing," and "Dispensing Complete." Each sub-state could have its own transitions and actions, allowing for more granular control and more precise modeling of the process. This hierarchical structure enhances understanding and reduces ambiguity—particularly beneficial when multiple developers collaborate on a single system.

Think of the implications for debugging. A detailed nested state model allows for far easier pinpointing of error locations. Instead of a broad "Dispensing Item" state failing, the error source may now be accurately identified to be “Verifying Dispensing” or “Initiating Dispensing”, leading to rapid and more precise debugging. Such targeted analysis reduces resolution times and minimizes software development costs.

Another valuable advanced technique is the use of hierarchical state machines. These machines build upon nested states by allowing you to encapsulate multiple state machines within each other. This is incredibly useful when modeling systems with significant independent components. Each component could be represented by its own state machine. For example, a vending machine might have separate state machines for the payment system, the item dispensing mechanism, and the network connectivity system. The overall system's state machine could then integrate these individual components, providing an overview of their interaction and collaboration.

These techniques improve modularity. The ability to model complex behavior in a hierarchical way leads to better code organization and promotes easier reuse and maintenance. This makes your code clearer and less susceptible to defects when updates or changes are applied.

Beyond nesting and hierarchy, consider the importance of well-defined events and actions. Avoid vague event names like "Error." Instead, use specific events such as "PaymentFailed," "ItemJam," or "NetworkDisconnected." Similarly, define actions clearly, specifying precisely what should happen in each state transition. Accurate event and action specifications reduce ambiguity and enhance the precision of your state machine model.

The use of guards adds further refinement. Guards are conditions that must be true for a transition to occur. For example, a transition from "Selecting Item" to "Dispensing Item" might have a guard of "Sufficient Funds." This ensures that the machine only dispenses an item if the customer has enough money, preventing unwanted behavior and improving the robustness of your model.

Furthermore, activities represent behaviors that persist while an object resides in a given state. These activities are not triggered by a specific event but continuously execute while the object remains in the state. For example, the vending machine's "Idle" state might have an activity that continuously monitors network connectivity or sensor inputs from the various internal mechanisms.

By carefully incorporating these advanced modeling techniques, your state machine diagrams will become far more accurate, comprehensive, and useful. They'll evolve from simple illustrations into powerful tools for designing, understanding, and maintaining complex software systems. This translates directly to improved software quality, reduced development costs, and enhanced project success rates—all vital objectives in today's agile environment. The ability to effectively model complex interactions with precision is paramount to creating effective and efficient software systems. The use of nested states, hierarchical state machines, well-defined events and actions, guards, and activities provides the tools to create state machines that accurately reflect even the most nuanced system behaviors. Remember that clear, precise modeling is not merely a best practice—it's a critical element of successful software engineering.

6 Agile Modeling Practices

Iteration planning in an Agile context isn't about creating a rigid, detailed plan upfront. Instead, it's about creating a flexible roadmap for the upcoming iteration, a short, time-boxed period of development, typically lasting one to four weeks. Begin by reviewing the product backlog, a prioritized list of features and functionalities. Identify the user stories that can realistically be completed within the iteration's timeframe. Remember, it's better to under-estimate than over-estimate. Collaboration is key here; the entire team – developers, testers, designers – should be involved in this estimation process. Using techniques like planning poker, the team can collectively agree on the effort and complexity of each story. This collaborative approach ensures everyone is on the same page and minimizes misunderstandings later on. Finally, document the plan, but keep it concise and easily adaptable. Changes are inevitable, and the plan should be a living document reflecting the team's progress and challenges.

Model-Driven Development (MDD) leverages UML models as the primary artifacts for software development. Unlike traditional approaches where coding is often the starting point, MDD places models at the center, driving the generation of code and tests. This approach doesn't necessarily mean completely eliminating manual coding; often, developers refine and enhance the automatically generated code. The benefits are significant. MDD promotes consistency and reduces errors, because the code is directly derived from the models. It also simplifies maintenance; changes made to the models are automatically reflected in the code. However, selecting the right modeling tools and establishing clear model-to-code transformation rules is vital for success. Careful consideration of your team's expertise and project specifics is crucial for a smooth transition to MDD. A phased implementation is often recommended, allowing the team to gradually integrate MDD into their workflow.

Continuous integration is more than just regularly integrating code; it's about establishing a continuous feedback loop. In an Agile environment using UML, this means frequently integrating the models and the generated (or manually written) code into a shared repository. Automated build processes should then be triggered, compiling the code and running unit and integration tests. This cycle ensures early detection of integration issues, preventing conflicts and reducing the risk of significant problems surfacing later in the development cycle. Tools like Jenkins or GitLab CI/CD greatly automate this process, freeing developers to focus on building features, rather than fixing broken builds. A well-defined continuous integration pipeline helps monitor the health of the software and fosters a proactive approach to quality assurance. Implementing continuous integration requires clear guidelines, automated testing strategies, and a commitment from the entire team to maintain the integrity of the codebase. The payoff is improved software quality and faster delivery cycles.

6.1 Iteration Planning

Effective iteration planning is crucial for success in Agile development. It's not just about scheduling tasks; it's about strategically aligning your team's efforts with the overall project goals, ensuring that each iteration delivers tangible value and progresses the project toward completion. Think of it as a roadmap for a short, focused journey, constantly refined based on feedback and actual progress.

Successful iteration planning hinges on clear communication and shared understanding. Your team needs a unified vision of the iteration's objectives. This involves more than just assigning tasks; it requires collaboratively defining the user stories or features targeted for completion within the iteration's timeframe. Visual aids, such as UML diagrams—specifically use case diagrams and sequence diagrams, can dramatically improve this collaborative process.

Estimating the effort required for each task is a critical, yet often underestimated, aspect of iteration planning. This isn't about precise time tracking; rather, it's about developing a realistic sense of how much work the team can accomplish within the fixed time constraints of an iteration. Utilize techniques like story point estimation, ensuring everyone is on the same page regarding the relative complexity of different tasks. Consistent calibration is key; regular reviews help the team refine their estimation abilities.

Prioritization is paramount. Not all tasks are created equal. Some may directly impact user value or resolve critical issues, while others may be less important. Use a prioritization framework like MoSCoW (Must have, Should have, Could have, Won't have) to systematically rank tasks based on their business value. This ensures the team focuses on high-value items first, maximizing the return on their effort during the iteration.

Risk assessment plays a crucial role in iterative development. Identify potential roadblocks or challenges that could derail progress during the iteration. Could you encounter technical difficulties? Are there dependencies on other teams or external factors? Proactive identification of these risks allows for mitigation strategies to be developed and integrated into the plan, ensuring smoother execution.

Regular progress monitoring is vital. Daily stand-up meetings or similar check-ins provide valuable opportunities to track progress, identify impediments, and make necessary adjustments to the plan. This isn't about micromanagement; rather, it's about fostering transparency and collaboration, enabling the team to respond quickly to unforeseen circumstances. The use of a Kanban board or a similar visual system can make progress monitoring more efficient and transparent.

Adaptability is the cornerstone of Agile methodology. Iteration planning should be a dynamic process, adapting to changing circumstances and new information. Don't be afraid to adjust the plan throughout the iteration. Regular reviews and retrospectives provide crucial feedback mechanisms to refine the planning process for future iterations.

Remember, successful iteration planning is an iterative process itself. As your team gains experience, it will refine its techniques and improve its estimation and planning capabilities. Learn from each iteration and continuously strive for improvement; this is fundamental to the iterative nature of agile development. Through consistent practice, effective communication, and a willingness to adapt, you can transform iteration planning from a procedural task into a strategic tool driving successful software development.

UML diagrams, specifically use-case and sequence diagrams, facilitate clear communication during the planning phase. Use-case diagrams help you visually represent user interactions and desired system functionalities, whilst sequence diagrams clarify the interaction between different system components. Employing these visual aids ensures that all stakeholders share a common understanding of the iteration's goals and the steps required to achieve them. This helps to mitigate miscommunications and ensures everyone is working towards the same objectives.

Integrating testing into the iteration plan is critical. Don't view testing as a separate phase; rather, incorporate it into the development cycle, ensuring that tests are designed and executed alongside development tasks. Agile methodologies emphasize continuous testing and integration, enabling early detection of defects and preventing them from accumulating and compounding.

Collaboration and teamwork are the foundations of agile development. Iteration planning is not a solitary activity, but a collaborative exercise involving the entire team. Encouraging open communication and shared ownership of the plan ensures that everyone understands their role and responsibilities. This promotes a sense of shared purpose and increases team morale, ultimately leading to a more efficient and effective development process. Remember to document all decisions and agreements, making the iteration plan a readily available reference for the entire team.

6.2 Model-Driven Development

Model-driven development (MDD) isn't about creating perfect, static models; it's about leveraging models throughout the entire software development lifecycle. Think of it as a powerful tool, not a rigid constraint. Your models evolve alongside your understanding of the system, reflecting changes and adaptations as you progress. This iterative process minimizes risks and keeps the project adaptable.

Unlike traditional methods that heavily rely on code-first approaches, MDD places the model at the center. This central model serves as a single source of truth, ensuring consistency between design, implementation, and documentation. Imagine a single, ever-updating blueprint that everyone on the team can access and understand. This transparency significantly improves communication and collaboration.

Implementing MDD within an agile framework requires careful consideration of your tools and team workflow. Selecting a robust modeling tool that seamlessly integrates with your development environment is crucial. You need tools that can generate code from the model, verify model consistency, and allow for model transformations as the project evolves. Choosing the right tools is more than just functionality; it's about ease of use and team acceptance.

Furthermore, successful MDD necessitates a skilled team that understands both agile methodologies and UML. Team training on the chosen modeling tool is a must, equipping everyone with the skills to create, modify, and utilize the central model effectively. The training shouldn't be a one-time event but an ongoing process, adapting as new tools and methodologies are introduced.

Effective communication is not merely about using the right tools; it's about fostering a collaborative environment where everyone understands the value of the model and its role in the project. Regular model reviews, where the team collectively examines the model for accuracy, consistency, and completeness, become essential to ensure the model remains a valuable asset rather than a liability.

The transition to MDD might initially seem challenging, but incremental adoption can ease the process. Begin by applying MDD to a small, well-defined part of the project. This allows the team to gain practical experience and identify potential challenges before scaling up. This gradual implementation minimizes disruption and enables continuous improvement.

Remember, MDD isn't a replacement for coding; instead, it's a powerful complement. The generated code provides a solid foundation, significantly reducing manual coding efforts. Developers still need to write custom code for certain parts, integrate external libraries, and address specific system requirements. However, MDD automates much of the tedious, repetitive work, freeing the developers to focus on more complex and challenging tasks.

Model transformations play a crucial role in the success of MDD. These transformations enable the automatic generation of code, documentation, and test cases from the model. The key lies in choosing the right transformation strategies to suit the project's needs and the complexities of the system being developed. This aspect often requires careful planning and consideration of different transformation approaches.

Continuous integration and continuous delivery (CI/CD) pipelines become integral components in a well-implemented MDD process. The pipelines automatically verify model consistency, generate code, run tests, and deploy the software. This automation ensures that changes to the model are immediately reflected in the running system, providing constant feedback and enhancing quality.

However, be aware of the potential downsides. Over-reliance on automated code generation may result in inflexible code that's hard to adapt. A balance is needed—leverage the benefits of automation but remain prepared to write custom code when it's necessary. Overly complex models can become unmanageable, hindering productivity rather than improving it. The model should be kept as simple as possible while capturing the essential aspects of the system.

6.3 Continuous Integration

Continuous integration is more than just a buzzword; it's a cornerstone of successful Agile development, especially when coupled with UML modeling. Think of it as a safety net, catching potential problems early and preventing them from snowballing into major headaches later in the development lifecycle. It's about constantly integrating code changes into a shared repository, frequently testing the resulting build, and rapidly identifying and resolving any integration issues. This proactive approach drastically reduces the risk of integration problems during later stages, resulting in smoother deployments and higher-quality software.

Implementing continuous integration effectively requires a well-defined process. Start by establishing a version control system, such as Git, as the central repository for your code. This provides a single source of truth, facilitating collaboration and tracking changes throughout the development process. Each developer should commit code changes regularly, ideally several times a day. Regular commits, coupled with a clear and concise commit message describing the change, ensures traceability and facilitates easy rollback if needed. This makes it far easier to pinpoint the source of integration issues should they arise.

Automated build processes are vital. You need a system capable of automatically compiling the code, running tests, and deploying the software upon successful completion of the build process. Tools like Jenkins, GitLab CI, or Azure DevOps provide a flexible framework for automating this process. Their user-friendly interfaces allow for simple configuration of build triggers, testing procedures, and deployment targets. This automation frees developers from tedious manual tasks, allowing them to focus on writing clean and functional code, accelerating the entire development process, and ultimately improving the overall software quality. A well-configured automated build pipeline acts as a guardian, ensuring that the latest code changes remain functional.

Thorough testing is paramount. Continuous integration hinges on the ability to quickly and reliably identify integration problems. This mandates a robust testing strategy incorporating unit, integration, and system tests. Unit tests verify the individual components of the software work as expected. Integration tests ensure the interaction between different components is correct. System tests validate that the entire system functions as designed. The more comprehensive your test suite, the more confidence you can have in the stability of your software. Automation also plays a crucial role here, with automated testing tools capable of executing tests frequently and reporting results automatically, leading to rapid identification of errors and bugs.

The connection between continuous integration and UML modeling lies in the way both facilitate early error detection and iterative refinement. A well-defined UML model serves as a blueprint for the software, making it easier to track the implementation against the design. By incorporating model-driven development practices, you can generate test cases directly from the model, ensuring that the code complies with the specified design. This allows for early identification of discrepancies, leading to more efficient problem resolution. Continuous integration, then, serves as a mechanism for verifying that the code implementation is faithful to the UML model, ensuring that the software adheres to its specifications.

Finally, remember that continuous integration is an iterative process. Start small and gradually introduce more sophisticated practices. Begin by implementing basic automated builds and unit tests. As your team gains experience and confidence, you can progressively expand the testing suite to encompass integration and system tests. It's a journey, not a destination, and continuous improvement is key to long-term success. Embrace change, actively seek feedback, and iterate on your CI/CD pipeline to refine your process and maximize its effectiveness. This continuous improvement loop is the key to building a robust and efficient software delivery pipeline, allowing for faster iterations and ultimately improving product quality and customer satisfaction. Don't be afraid to experiment and adapt your practices to your unique environment and team dynamic. The goal is to streamline the development process and build more reliable and high-quality software.

7 Conclusion and Future Trends

Agile methodologies, such as Scrum and Kanban, have revolutionized software development, emphasizing iterative development and collaborative teamwork. Their focus on flexibility and responsiveness to changing requirements perfectly complements the visual clarity of UML. The iterative nature of Agile aligns seamlessly with the incremental approach to model creation and refinement inherent in UML's design. This synergy enables teams to quickly adapt to evolving needs, ensuring the software remains relevant and aligned with business goals throughout its lifecycle. Effective implementation necessitates a deep understanding of both Agile principles and the strengths of UML diagrams.

Scaling Agile for larger projects poses unique challenges. Traditional Agile approaches, while effective for smaller teams, can become unwieldy when dealing with hundreds or even thousands of developers. Scaled Agile Frameworks (SAFe), Large-Scale Scrum (LeSS), and Disciplined Agile Delivery (DAD) address this issue by providing structures and methodologies to manage complex projects effectively. These frameworks integrate UML effectively, allowing for clear communication and coordination across multiple teams and geographical locations. Mastering these frameworks significantly expands the applicability of both Agile and UML to large-scale, complex software systems.

Emerging UML practices continue to evolve, adapting to the needs of modern software development. The integration of UML with model-driven architecture (MDA) and model transformation tools offers opportunities for automation and increased efficiency. These tools facilitate the automated generation of code from UML models, reducing manual effort and minimizing the risk of errors. Furthermore, the use of UML profiles, which customize UML for specific domains, is growing, enhancing the expressiveness and suitability of UML in niche areas such as embedded systems or medical device development. Staying abreast of these advancements is crucial for leveraging the full potential of UML in modern development environments.

Beyond UML and Agile, several best practices significantly enhance the efficiency and effectiveness of software development. Continuous integration and continuous delivery (CI/CD) pipelines automate the build, test, and deployment process, resulting in faster feedback loops and quicker releases. Test-driven development (TDD) ensures code quality through rigorous testing from the initial design stages. Pair programming and code reviews, hallmarks of Agile, promote knowledge sharing and reduce defects. The seamless integration of these techniques with UML modeling creates a potent combination for building high-quality software efficiently and effectively. The combined use of UML's visual clarity with these agile best practices offers superior development outcomes.

The future of UML and Agile methodologies appears bright, with both continuing to evolve and adapt to the changing landscape of software development. The increasing complexity of software systems, the rise of cloud computing, and the growing adoption of DevOps practices will continue to drive innovation in both fields. We can expect further advancements in model-driven engineering, the integration of UML with AI-powered tools, and the development of more sophisticated Agile frameworks. The continued collaboration between UML and Agile experts will ensure that software development continues to adapt and meet the ever-evolving needs of the industry. Continuous learning and adaptation are essential for remaining at the forefront of this dynamic field. Mastering these methodologies and keeping up-to-date with the latest developments will ensure you thrive as a software developer.

7.1 Agile Methodologies

Agile methodologies prioritize iterative development, fostering flexibility and adaptability throughout the software development lifecycle. This contrasts sharply with traditional waterfall approaches, where each phase must be completed before the next begins, leading to inflexibility and potential for significant rework later on. Instead, Agile embraces change, viewing it not as a threat, but as an opportunity for improvement. This iterative approach allows for continuous feedback incorporation, resulting in a final product that more closely aligns with the evolving needs of the client and market conditions. The inherent flexibility of Agile methods reduces the risk of project failure.

The core values of Agile are enshrined in the Agile Manifesto, which emphasizes individuals and interactions over processes and tools; working software over comprehensive documentation; customer collaboration over contract negotiation; and responding to change over following a plan. These principles guide the development process, ensuring a focus on delivering value quickly and efficiently. While documentation is important, Agile prioritizes working software, recognizing that the most valuable form of documentation is the code itself. This doesn't mean neglecting documentation entirely; instead, it calls for creating just enough documentation to effectively support development. The iterative nature of Agile allows for continuous adaptation, ensuring that the team remains responsive to changing requirements.

Several popular Agile frameworks exist, each with its own unique approach. Scrum, for instance, utilizes short iterations called sprints (typically two to four weeks), with daily stand-up meetings to track progress and identify potential roadblocks. Kanban, on the other hand, focuses on visualizing workflow and limiting work in progress, enabling efficient task management and quicker delivery. Extreme Programming (XP) prioritizes simplicity, communication, feedback, and courage, emphasizing technical excellence and relentless improvement. Each framework provides a structured approach to managing the development process while maintaining the core values of the Agile Manifesto. Selecting the right framework depends on the specific project requirements and team dynamics. You might find that hybrid approaches, combining elements from multiple frameworks, are the most effective for your team's context.

Agile methodologies greatly benefit from the use of UML (Unified Modeling Language) diagrams. While the Agile Manifesto emphasizes working software over comprehensive documentation, UML diagrams provide a valuable visual language for communicating design decisions and clarifying complex interactions within the system. This enhanced communication improves team collaboration and allows for quicker feedback. Use cases, for instance, help to clearly define the functionalities from the user's perspective. Class diagrams provide a structured overview of the system's components, allowing for a clearer understanding of relationships between different parts. Sequence diagrams visually represent the flow of messages between objects, helping to identify potential bottlenecks or inconsistencies in the design. These models can be revisited and updated throughout the iterative development process, ensuring the software stays in line with the changing requirements.

Integrating UML into an Agile workflow requires careful planning and execution. It's crucial to avoid creating overly detailed or complex models that consume excessive time and effort. The goal is to create just-enough models to support the current iteration and effectively communicate design decisions within the team. Tools like visual modeling software can automate tasks and help streamline the process. The focus should always be on achieving the objectives of the current iteration, not on achieving perfect models. The models should be viewed as living documents, constantly evolving to reflect the progress of the project and feedback received from stakeholders. Remember that the primary goal is to build working software, and UML is a tool to help achieve this goal. Overly complex UML will ultimately undermine Agile's principles of simplicity and speed. Ultimately, the use of UML tools and techniques within an Agile framework can substantially improve the efficiency and clarity of the development process.

7.2 Scaling Agile

Scaling Agile methodologies requires careful consideration of organizational structure, team dynamics, and communication strategies. It's not simply a matter of applying Agile principles at a larger scale; instead, it demands a thoughtful approach to adapt the framework to the unique challenges of a larger enterprise. Successful scaling relies on establishing a clear vision, aligning teams around common goals, and implementing robust processes that facilitate collaboration and transparency across different teams and departments. This ensures everyone is working towards the same objectives, preventing potential conflicts and redundancies.

One key aspect involves creating a well-defined organizational structure. This means identifying clear roles and responsibilities, establishing lines of communication, and determining how teams will interact.

Consider frameworks like SAFe (Scaled Agile Framework) or LeSS (Large-Scale Scrum), each providing different approaches for structuring and organizing large Agile projects. These frameworks help you navigate the complexities of coordinating multiple teams, ensuring that they work efficiently and collaboratively towards a shared objective, leading to a more streamlined development process. Choosing the right framework, however, needs to be driven by the specific context of your organization and the project.

Effective communication is paramount. As the number of teams and individuals involved in a project increases, the complexity of communication also rises. Therefore, it's critical to implement systems that facilitate clear, concise, and timely communication. Tools like collaborative project management software can be invaluable in this regard. Regular meetings, stand-ups, and other communication channels help to keep everyone informed, promoting transparency and preventing misunderstandings. These practices are instrumental in maintaining the Agile spirit of collaboration and transparency within a larger organizational structure. This ensures that information flows freely among team members and stakeholders, ultimately contributing to a successful project outcome.

Furthermore, you should not neglect the role of leadership. Effective leadership is critical for the success of any Agile initiative, and this is even more crucial when scaling Agile to larger projects. Leaders need to foster a culture of collaboration, trust, and continuous improvement, emphasizing shared responsibility and empowering teams to make decisions. They should promote a culture of learning and experimentation, encouraging teams to try new approaches and adapt their strategies as needed, always keeping a focus on continuous improvement. Effective leaders will champion the Agile philosophy, enabling team members to embrace its principles and work collaboratively.

To successfully scale Agile, continuous improvement is paramount. Regular retrospectives should be conducted to evaluate the effectiveness of the current practices and to identify areas for improvement. This requires a commitment to actively seeking feedback from all team members and stakeholders, including customers and end-users. The insights gathered from these retrospectives can inform adjustments to processes and practices, ensuring that the Agile framework continually adapts to the evolving needs of the project. This helps to minimize risks, improve efficiency, and optimize the overall development process.

A major challenge in scaling Agile is maintaining the agility and responsiveness that are hallmarks of the methodology. While structure and processes are crucial for larger projects, it's critical to avoid introducing excessive bureaucracy or rigidity. The goal is to find a balance between well-defined structures that facilitate collaboration and processes that support flexibility and responsiveness. This balance ensures that the benefits of Agile – adaptability, speed, and efficiency – are preserved even as the scale of the project increases. Therefore, continuous monitoring and refinement of these processes are necessary for optimal performance and adapting to new circumstances.

Finally, remember that scaling Agile is a journey, not a destination. There is no one-size-fits-all solution; the best approach will depend on your specific organizational context. The key is to start small, experiment with different approaches, and continuously adapt your strategy based on your experiences and learnings. Embrace the iterative nature of Agile and use the feedback gained to refine your scaling strategy. This ensures that the Agile framework remains responsive to your unique needs, ultimately leading to a successful outcome. This constant refinement is essential for long-term success in scaling Agile projects.

7.3 Emerging UML Practices

The increasing complexity of modern software systems demands more sophisticated UML practices. While traditional UML diagrams remain valuable, adapting them to agile methodologies requires a nuanced approach. We need to move beyond simply creating static diagrams; instead, we should leverage UML to support the iterative and incremental nature of agile development. This entails using UML not as a rigid upfront design specification, but as a living, evolving model that adapts as the project progresses.

One key adaptation involves embracing lightweight modeling techniques. Instead of striving for all-encompassing, excessively detailed diagrams early on, focus on creating high-level models first. These initial models should capture the core functionality and architecture. Detail can be added incrementally, during subsequent iterations, as the understanding of the system evolves. This iterative approach helps avoid wasted effort on modeling details that might change later. It also ensures the model remains relevant and useful throughout the project lifecycle. Remember, the goal is not a perfect model but a useful one that helps the team communicate and collaborate effectively.

Another vital shift is towards model-driven development (MDD). In agile projects, the model becomes a central artifact, not just a supporting document. With MDD, the UML model directly drives the implementation, enabling developers to generate code, tests, and other artifacts directly from the model. This tight integration minimizes discrepancies between the design and the implementation, enhancing code quality and reducing rework. Tools supporting MDD greatly accelerate development and allow for increased agility. Adopting such tools and techniques should be part of any strategy focused on improving software development efficiency. This is a shift from documentation to active participation in the development process.

Furthermore, effective communication and collaboration are pivotal. UML diagrams, by their visual nature, facilitate communication among developers, stakeholders, and clients. Regular reviews of the UML models within the agile sprints provide opportunities for feedback and continuous improvement. Consider using collaborative modeling tools that allow multiple team members to work on the models simultaneously, enhancing real-time discussions and promoting shared understanding.

Open communication throughout the entire software development process is a crucial factor for project success.

The integration of UML with other agile practices, such as test-driven development (TDD) and behavior-driven development (BDD), is also crucial. UML diagrams can be used to visually represent test cases and scenarios, making them easier to understand and maintain. This approach leads to more robust and comprehensive testing, reducing bugs and improving software quality. By effectively combining UML modeling with existing agile best practices, the power of each is amplified.

Finally, consider the use of specialized UML profiles to tailor the modeling language to specific needs. This could be for domain-specific modeling, such as modeling financial transactions or medical devices, or for specific development platforms and technologies. These profiles will help you extend the usability of UML diagrams in different fields. Using tailored profiles could lead to a decrease in misunderstandings and a greater efficiency in using UML. By constantly refining and adjusting UML models to accommodate new insights and feedback, teams can use UML to create high-quality software products efficiently. This flexible approach is a key driver of success in agile projects. Always adapt, always improve, and focus on the project's goals. By focusing on these emerging practices, the use of UML in agile settings can evolve past simply a documentation tool to a central component of the software development lifecycle.

7.4 Software Development Best Practices

Effective software development hinges on a robust set of best practices, significantly enhancing project success and developer satisfaction. These practices aren't merely suggestions; they're crucial for building high-quality, maintainable, and scalable software. Following these guidelines is paramount for beginners navigating the complexities of software creation.

Prioritize code readability above all else. Clean, well-commented code is significantly easier to understand, debug, and maintain. Imagine yourself returning to a project six months later – you'll thank your past self for the clarity. Consistent formatting, meaningful variable names, and concise functions are key components of this readability. Use tools like linters and formatters to enforce these standards, preventing stylistic inconsistencies that can hinder collaboration and comprehension. Thorough commenting clarifies the purpose and functionality of different code sections, aiding in future comprehension and modifications. Remember, code isn't just for the machine; it's for human understanding too. Neglecting readability is an avoidable pitfall that can lead to significant difficulties later. Consider the long-term maintainability of your code; if you don't understand it in a few months, how can you expect others to?

Version control is indispensable. Using Git (or a similar system) allows you to track changes, collaborate effectively, and revert to previous versions if necessary. This is more than just a backup; it's a safety net and a collaborative tool. Imagine the frustration of losing several hours of work due to a simple mistake—version control prevents such catastrophic incidents. Branching strategies streamline collaborative development, enabling simultaneous work on features without interfering with the main codebase. Regular commits, with meaningful commit messages, provide a clear history of project development, significantly simplifying debugging and understanding the evolution of the code. Think of your version control as a detailed journal of your project, a resource you'll consult often, so keep it organized and well-documented.

Test-driven development (TDD) significantly improves software quality. By writing tests before the actual code, you define the expected behavior and ensure that your implementation meets those specifications. This approach seems counterintuitive at first, but it promotes a more modular and structured development process, resulting in more robust and reliable software. This allows early detection of bugs and prevents issues from escalating as the project progresses. Unit tests, integration tests, and system tests should form part of a comprehensive testing strategy, providing a range of verification levels to check the code at every possible stage. Moreover, having a comprehensive test suite simplifies the debugging process significantly and allows for more confident refactoring without fear of unintended consequences.

Agile methodologies emphasize iterative development and continuous feedback. This approach fosters flexibility and adaptability, allowing for quick adjustments to changing requirements. In short, Agile allows you to refine your product incrementally, reacting to user feedback and market needs. This flexibility allows faster integration of user feedback and a final product that better satisfies user needs and expectations. This adaptability is particularly crucial in today's fast-paced development landscape where needs and requirements are often in constant flux. Remember that a fixed, rigid development model can lead to significant project overruns and a product that fails to meet user expectations.

Effective communication is critical. Frequent team meetings, clear documentation, and open channels for feedback are essential for successful collaboration. This proactive approach helps prevent misunderstandings and keeps everyone on the same page. Regular stand-up meetings allow everyone to communicate updates and roadblocks efficiently. While the technical skills are paramount, effective communication within the team, as well as with stakeholders, is also crucial to ensuring that everyone works efficiently towards the same goal, thus, preventing delays and misinterpretations. This smooth exchange of information enables everyone to stay up-to-date and provides opportunities to address issues before they escalate. Document your code, your design choices, and your assumptions for future reference.

Employ code reviews as a means of quality assurance and knowledge sharing. Having another pair of eyes on your code can uncover hidden bugs and offer valuable insights into improvements. This collaborative process can improve the code's quality and helps junior developers learn from more experienced colleagues. Code reviews aren't just about finding bugs; they're about fostering a culture of collaboration and knowledge transfer within the team, improving overall code quality, and promoting a better understanding of coding style and best practices. They also help create a more robust codebase, less prone to errors and easier to maintain over time. Remember this is a learning opportunity for everyone involved.

7.5 Future of UML and Agile

The synergy between UML and Agile methodologies is not just a passing trend; it's a fundamental shift in how software is conceived and built. While Agile prioritizes iterative development and adaptability, UML provides the visual language to structure and communicate the design effectively. This powerful combination is here to stay, constantly evolving to meet the demands of increasingly complex projects.

Agile's emphasis on rapid iteration and feedback loops demands a modeling approach equally flexible. Rigid, upfront design processes simply don't work within the iterative nature of Agile; UML, however, is adaptable enough to facilitate these quick adjustments. We can leverage UML's power to create models that evolve alongside the project, not hindering but enabling the velocity of development. Therefore, mastering UML becomes a strategic advantage in the agile context, enabling teams to quickly visualize and communicate changes, leading to a significantly reduced risk of misunderstandings and costly rework.

Consider the scenario of a team employing Scrum. Each sprint requires detailed planning, identifying the tasks needed to reach a sprint goal. UML diagrams, specifically use case diagrams and sequence diagrams, help visualize these tasks and their interactions. This shared understanding ensures the team focuses its energy efficiently, reducing conflicts and improving overall productivity. The iterative nature of sprints means these diagrams themselves are subject to refinements and adjustments as the sprint progresses, illustrating UML's responsiveness.

Beyond the core Agile frameworks, the landscape of software development is constantly evolving. New technologies and architectural patterns demand a modeling language capable of keeping pace. UML, with its extensible nature and the ongoing development of profiles and tools, proves itself incredibly versatile, adapting to these new challenges. We can anticipate continued development of UML in areas such as microservices architecture and cloud-native applications, making UML a crucial tool in any modern software development toolkit.

The integration of UML tools with existing Agile project management platforms is another exciting avenue. Tools that allow seamless transition between modeling and coding are already emerging, bridging the gap between design and implementation. This seamless integration will improve efficiency, reducing the administrative overhead often associated with different tools. This, in turn, allows developers to focus on building software, not navigating between different systems.

However, the future isn't without its challenges. One concern remains the adoption and training required for wider UML proficiency within Agile teams. In the current landscape, some Agile teams might not fully utilize the potential of UML modeling. Promoting UML training and demonstrating its tangible benefits to the project lifecycle is paramount for unlocking its full potential in an Agile workflow. Moreover, encouraging the use of UML as a collaborative tool, not a solitary endeavor, can further streamline the process.

Looking ahead, the continued success of UML in the Agile world relies on its ability to remain relevant and adaptable to technological advancements. The development of standardized profiles for specific domains, such as IoT or AI, can make UML even more accessible and valuable across industries. This proactive approach will help to reduce the learning curve for developers, ensuring UML continues to be adopted and understood by the larger community. This ensures its continued utility, not merely as a documentation tool, but as a vital element in the overall Agile development process.

In conclusion, the future of UML within the Agile paradigm is bright. Its versatility, adaptability, and ongoing development ensure its continued relevance. However, a focus on training, integration, and standardisation is vital to realize the full potential of this powerful combination. The successful integration of UML and Agile hinges on a deep understanding of both methodologies and the willingness to embrace collaborative modeling practices. By strategically utilizing UML diagrams, teams can enhance transparency, reduce risk, and ultimately, deliver higher-quality software faster. The future is about optimizing this synergy, not simply using UML as an add-on, but integrating it as an intrinsic part of the Agile workflow. The result? An efficient and effective development process, delivering exceptional products to market with greater speed and lower risk. This ensures not only the survival of UML, but its crucial role in the ever-evolving landscape of Agile software development. This harmonious pairing positions developers and enterprises to navigate the complexities of modern software creation.

www.ingramcontent.com/pod-product-compliance
Lightning Source LLC
LaVergne TN
LVHW022013200926
848481LV00007B/2371

* 9 7 9 8 3 4 8 5 9 7 7 7 1 *